Series 606B

A Ladybird 'Easy-Reading' book

'People at Work'

THE CAR MAKERS

by I. & J. HAVENHAND

with illustrations by
JOHN BERRY

Publishers: Ladybird Books Ltd . Loughborough

Printed in England

THE CAR MAKERS

Motor cars were first made in England just before 1900. The parts for the bodies and engines were hand made, and the cars built from these one at a time. This took a long time and the cars cost a lot of money.

Some of these old cars, like the one shown opposite, are still running and every year take part in a race from London to Brighton.

The car makers had to find a quicker and cheaper way of making cars so that more people could buy them.

7214 0074 4

258
DLH 202

Instead of making all the parts at their own works, some car makers asked other firms to do this. The parts were only fitted together by the car makers.

An American named Henry Ford found a quick way of making cars. He had a gang of men who fitted together each part of a car. Then the men moved on to another car. Other men brought the parts to them.

When the cars were finished they were driven away and another line of cars was started.

To-day, the cars are carried by a moving track. This is quicker than having men move to the cars.

Modern car-making works are so large that each one is really a lot of factories close together. Thousands of men and women work in each factory, making and assembling the many different parts of cars.

As well as factories there are blocks of offices. Men and girls work in these, taking in orders for cars and planning the work in the factories. Their work is just as important as that of the men who make the cars.

While the workmen are making thousands of new cars every week, other men are busy planning new models.

When it is decided to change to a new model, a lot of extra work has to be done in the offices and factories. Many alterations have to be made to the machinery in the factories. Even factories a long way away might have to make alterations if they are to supply parts for the new model.

The change-over to a new model can cost as much as two million pounds.

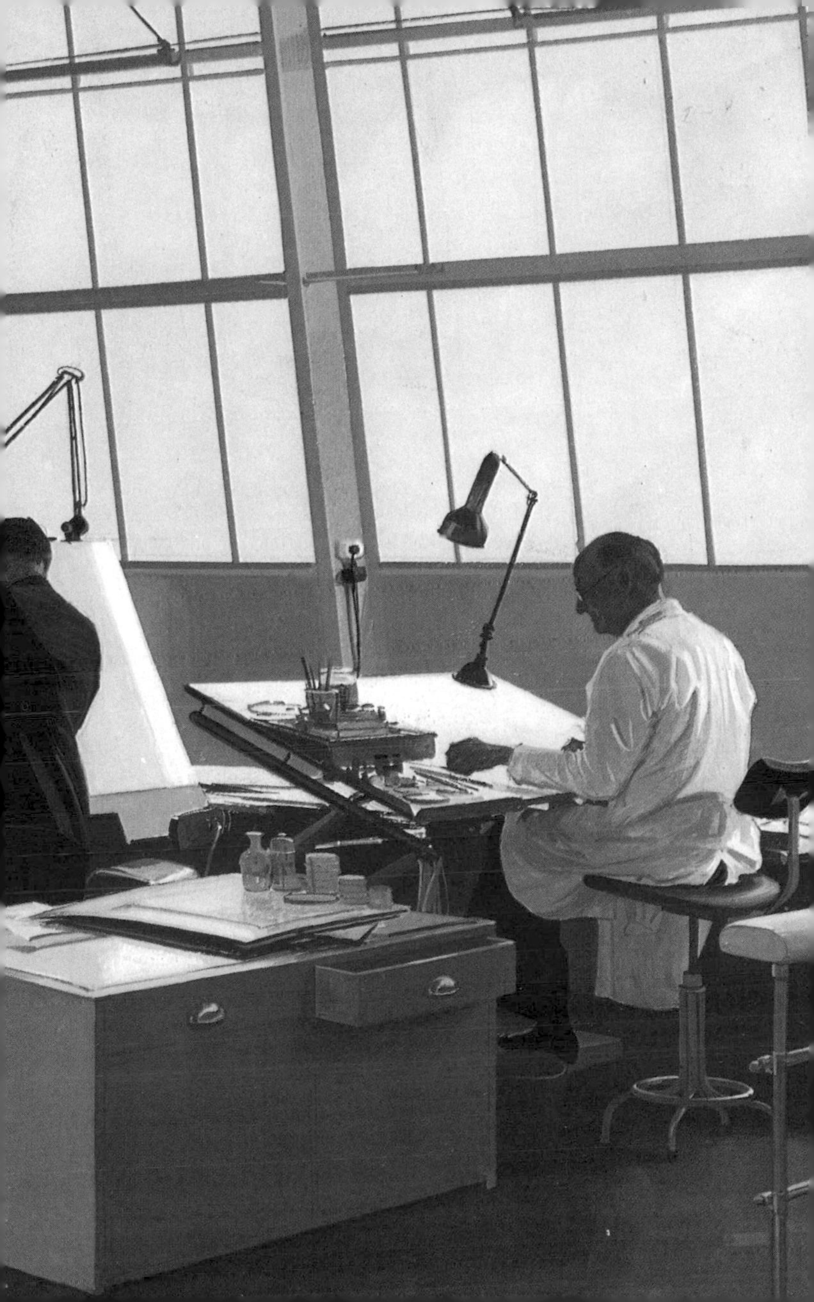

Engineers try to make better engines and better brakes. Designers think about what the outside and inside of the cars will look like. They make drawings of different looking cars.

Before a new car is built, small clay models are made. After this, a full size 'mock-up' of the car is made of wood.

When everyone agrees about the 'mock-up', a full size car is made. This is called a 'prototype'. The prototype is tested and changed until it satisfies the designers.

The new car is kept a secret all this time. The only people who see it are those working on it.

Many of the machines which make parts for the car engines do not need men to work them. They are called automatic transfer machines. These are really many machines all working together in a line.

A piece of metal is automatically loaded on to the machine. Grooves are cut, holes are drilled and over a hundred things may be done as the metal is automatically moved along.

A man stands by the control panel to see that the machine is working properly. If any part of an automatic transfer machine goes wrong the whole machine stops.

C
14

The bodies of the cars are made of thin sheets of steel. The steel sheets are first cut into flat shapes. These are automatically fed into huge presses which form them into roofs, mudguards, doors and other body parts.

There is a pressing machine for each part of the body. In the body factory there may be more than two hundred presses working together. All the different presses make the correct number of parts for complete car bodies.

The pressed parts are then sent on to be joined together.

When the pieces of a car body are joined together, men called welders do this. They use very hot flames that melt metal. The bodies travel along a moving track and pieces are welded on as they move along.

The welders wear dark goggles. These protect their eyes, which would be damaged if they looked at the bright flame.

Rough patches are made smooth by men using grinding wheels. The bodies are then bare, metal shells which have to be made ready for painting.

Before the car bodies can be painted, grease must be removed from them. After this, the metal is made rustproof and given a first coat of special paint called primer.

All this is done automatically. The car bodies are fixed to a machine which turns them over and over. They move along on an overhead track which passes above large tanks of liquid.

The bodies are lowered into each tank and are turned over a few times. This makes sure that all parts of the car bodies are protected against rust.

At the end of the track all the car bodies are the colour of dark chocolate. They are then ready to be painted. Men have to do this.

The men use spray guns to put on the coloured, finishing paint. They work in a specially made tunnel. Air is blown into the tunnel so that the men do not breathe in the fine paint spray. This would make them ill and damage their lungs.

The painted car bodies then pass into large ovens. The heat bakes on the paint and makes it very hard.

At the end of the paint-track the car bodies pass some electronic eyes. These electronic eyes are like beams of light. As the car bodies pass these beams, steel arms move out and grip them. The car bodies are then lifted up to another track.

This overhead track carries the car bodies to storage tracks up near the roof. They are kept there until they are needed on the assembly lines.

The assembly lines are where all the bits and pieces that make a car are fitted together.

The engine-making workshop may be a long way from the assembly line. At one car factory the engines are carried to the assembly line along an underground tunnel.

The tunnel is brightly lit and has six overhead carrying tracks. Three of these tracks carry engines and three carry back the empty engine holders.

While they are still underground, the engines are taken into large storage bays. When they are needed, the engines are automatically taken out and lifted up to the level of the assembly line.

Many of the smaller parts for the cars are made at other factories. Parts such as windows, door handles, speedometers and wheels with the tyres on are brought to the factory in large trailers. Men driving fork-lift carrying-trucks unload the parts.

All the bits and pieces that make each car are collected together by men and women. The parts are put in large metal trays, called palettes, and stacked ready for the assembly line.

All the parts that come in on one day are used up on the next.

28

Car orders from all over the world are collected at one office. These orders are sorted by girls using machines called computers.

Girls in the office use a machine called a teleprinter to send printed messages to the storage bays. Workmen start the car parts moving towards the assembly line. The correct body, engine and palette of parts all meet there.

A man gives out metal plates with the engine and body numbers on them. The numbers are the same as those on the order sheet. These plates are fixed on the car.

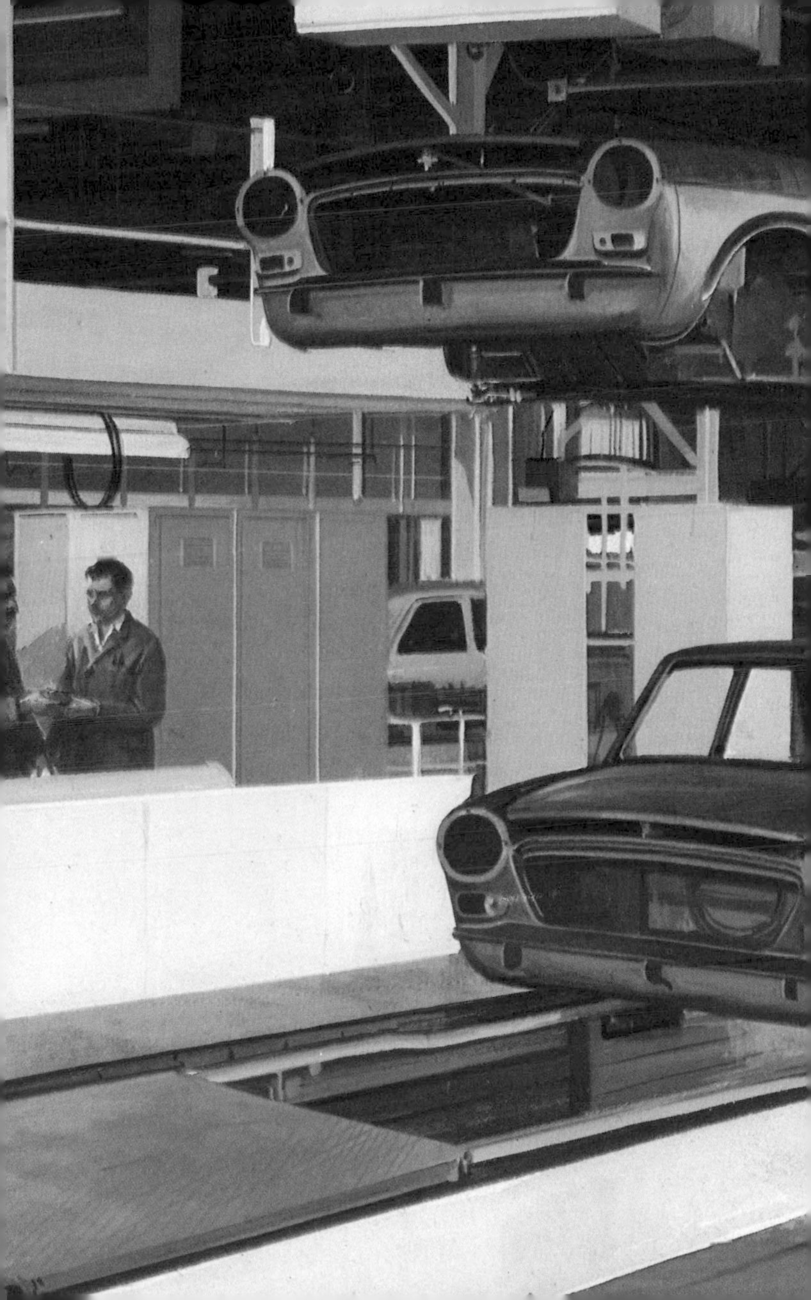

The car bodies are put on a moving track called the trim-line. As the bodies move slowly along, groups of men put in the fittings.

One group puts in the dash-boards. The bodies then move on to another group of men who put in the windows. Another group puts in the steering gear and the rest of the parts are fixed by other men. Each group fits in a few parts.

The power tools that the men use are driven by compressed air. At the end of the trim-line, the bodies have been fitted with all their parts.

At the side of the trim-line there is another moving track called the sub-frame assembly line. On this track groups of men build up the bottom part of the car. They also fix in the engine.

The palette, with all the parts for the car, moves along in between the two tracks.

At the end of the trim-line and the sub-frame assembly line, the two parts of the car are lifted up. They are carried overhead to a third track. This is the finishing track.

The finishing track runs above floor level so that some men can work underneath the cars and others work inside them. On this track the car bodies and the bottom parts of the cars are joined.

Men put on the wheels. These have come from the tyre makers and the tyres are already blown up. Other men connect the controls from inside the car to the engine and the brakes.

The end of the finishing track slopes down to floor level. There, a group of men takes over the cars for testing.

As the cars come off the finishing track, men put oil in the engine, water in the radiator and petrol in the tank.

A man gets into the driving seat, presses the starter and the car starts. Nearly all the cars, which are made from hundreds of parts, start at the first try.

The cars are driven onto rollers and tested as if they were on the road. They are tested at all speeds. After this the cars are driven down the workshop. The brakes are put on quickly to see that they work properly.

The speeds of all the moving tracks in the workshops are controlled by a computer. This makes sure that all the parts for the cars are at the right place when they are needed.

A man in a control room can see if all the tracks are working properly. He looks at a large glass screen on the wall. On this screen is a plan of the tracks. Each track is lit in a different colour.

If a track stops, the man can see where the trouble is and have it put right.

If the men who test the cars find anything wrong, they send the cars to another part of the workshop. After these cars have been put right, they are given another test on the road.

When new models are first made, a few of them are taken to the Motor Industry Research Association (M.I.R.A.) Testing Centre. There the cars are driven over very rough roads. They are taken through a dust tunnel and driven through water splashes. This is to make sure that the cars will work properly in any part of the world.

When the cars are finished they are ready to be sent to the car dealers who sell them.

Sometimes the cars are driven away. Some are taken to a collecting centre and put on special car-carrying trains. Most of the cars are taken away on car transporters. One driver can take away eight cars, or more, if he has a transporter with a trailer.

The cars made at a car factory are not all sold in this country. British cars are sold in nearly every country in the world.

AUSTIN
043 NE

Cars that are made for other countries are not the same as ours. The steering wheel and controls are on the left-hand side. The lights are different and special glass may have been fitted.

Many of the cars have to be taken a long way by sea. Men give these cars a thin coat of wax to protect the body from the sea air.

Some cars that go to other countries are not fitted together. The parts of the cars are sent in large, wooden boxes. These parts are put together when they arrive.

AUSTIN
AUSTIN
AUSTIN

Although a lot of work in a car factory is done by automatic machines, thousands of men and women work there.

These workers need tea-breaks and dinner-breaks. In the workshops there are automatic machines which serve tea, coffee and cold drinks.

At dinner-time all the assembly lines stop. The men and women go to one of the canteens where they can buy dinners. Some of the workers take sandwiches and eat them in the workshops. After the dinner-break all the tracks and machines start working again.

As more and more cars use the roads, the car makers try to make their cars safer to drive. Soon all cars will be fitted with seat belts, and doors that do not burst open in crashes. They will have steering columns that fold up and double sets of brakes.

To try out these things, new cars with dummy figures in them are crashed at a special testing ground.

No matter how safe cars are made, all who use the roads must take care. Drivers of cars and people who walk, adults and children as well, must all help to make the roads safe.

Series 606B